Action Learning, Action Research Association Ltd
Monograph Series

No. 8

Multiple, creative, methods for 'giving voice' in Alternative Education

Lara Fair, Lydia Gray, Damien Fogarty, Thelo Meleisea, Judy Bruce, Eileen Piggot-Irvine, Adrian Schoone and Hana Turner-Adams

Published by

Action Learning, Action Research Association Ltd

(https://www.alarassociation.org/publications)

2023

Communication: Dr Judy Bruce, University of Canterbury, NZ.

judy.bruce@canterbury.ac.nz

Biographical Statement

Lara Fair

I am a primary trained teacher and I have been working in Alternative Education style settings since graduating in 2001. I have worked with young people of all ages, in New Zealand (NZ) and in the United Kingdom (UK). The opportunity to be part of this action research has deepened my connection to this work. I felt very privileged to hear and share the stories of our young people. It also reinforced my passion for supporting them to reach their full potential.

Lydia Gray

I am a pedagogical leader and tutor at Waitakere Alternative Education Consortium in Auckland, NZ. I am a primary trained teacher who has a passion for working with at risk youth and have been working in Alternative Education for 7 years. I feel strongly about ensuring young people who have been disengaged from mainstream education are given a voice as this empowers them to feel seen, heard and valued. This is my first time being involved in action research and I have loved hearing the voice that has resonated out of our young people. I believe that what has been shared has the power provoke thought, spark action, and evoke change.

Damien Fogarty

I am a Pedagogical Leader with ACES (Auckland City Education Services) Alternative Education. I have been involved in working with rangatahi outside of a mainstream education setting for nearly 20 years. My passion is to see rangatahi empowered to achieve their potential through the unconditional support of significant adults in their lives, including Teachers. I have loved my first experience with action research and I have loved using talanoa as a research approach that is authentic and rewarding.

Thelo Meleisea

I came from a corporate background (15 years in the Finance industry) into AE in 2016. When the managers of Creative Learning Scheme (CLS) saw my CV and leadership background, I was asked to become CLS Campus Leader for Avondale in 2017. I worked as a Campus Leader for ACES from 2020 to beginning of 2022. I am now working as Community Liaison and transitioning into running my own business. I am a proud Samoan, married to a beautiful Ngā Puhi/Ngāti Porou wife, Mereana.

Judy Bruce

I am a Research Associate with the University of Canterbury, New Zealand. Based in Auckland, I am also Associate with the Leadership Lab, where I work as an education consultant. My areas of research and consultancy are in the fields of education innovation and equity.

Eileen Piggot-Irvine

I am an Adjunct Professor, Royal Roads University, Canada. I have been passionate about action research for over 20 years and led or been a participant in multiple projects across the globe. My goal in action research is to support others to understand and employ an approach which deeply honours the involvement, development and improvement of others in their role. The project described in this paper was focused on 'giving voice' to students. My goal was to also give voice to and honour the teachers.

Adrian Schoone

I am a senior lecturer in Education at Auckland University of Technology. My research focuses on educational opportunity and access for disenfranchised students. I have been involved in Alternative Education for over 20 years in various roles including as a teacher, AE provider manager, chairperson of the national body, and now researcher.

Hana Turner-Adams

I am a lecturer in Education at Waipapa Taumata Rau| The University of Auckland. My research focuses on students and teachers' experiences in education and the achievement disparities between Māori and non-Māori. The AE teachers' creativity in this project has been inspiring, and it's been a privilege to work alongside them and learn together about what is possible with action research.

Table of Contents

Biographical Statement 3
Abstract 7
Introduction 9
Alternative Education 9
Action research design 10
The multiple methods employed 12
    Lara Fair: Photovoice method 13
        Why this method? 13
        What I did 14
        My opinion of the process and outcomes 16
    Lydia Gray: Journal Writing 17
        Why this method 17
        What I did 17
        What worked 18
        What did not work or impeded the use of the method 18
        My opinions on this method 19
    Damien Fogarty: Talanoa 20
        A brief definition and summary of the approach 20
        The way the talanoa was conducted 20
        Challenges 21
        Why talanoa was useful 22
    Thelo Meleisea: Photo voice and 'go-along' place-based interviews 24
        Why these methods? 24
        What I did 24
        My opinion of the method 26
Conclusion 27
Funding details 29
Disclosure statement 29
References 29

Tables and Figures

Figure 1: Action Research Design 12
Figure 2: Example Student Chronology 15
Figure 3: Lydia's class at work 19
Figure 4: Damien in a talanoa session 23
Figure 5: An image collected by the student... 26

Abstract

Four data collection methods (photovoice, go-along interviews, journaling and talanoa) are described that were employed by teachers in an Alternative Education (AE) setting in New Zealand to collect stories of, and more deeply understand, previous unsuccessful schooling experiences and aspirations of our students. AE is often a last chance option for students who have been excluded from mainstream schools. Choices of methods for collecting stories were largely determined by the students' ability to 'give voice' to enable them to feel safe in telling their own stories. The stories collection was part of action research (AR) Reconnaissance Phase (current situation prior to implementation of improvements) data collection designed to ultimately create improved teaching and learning experiences. The content of the stories themselves and outcomes of improvement in teaching and learning are outlined in subsequent papers. The focus of this paper is solely on employment of methods from our perspective as teachers and it is written in our voice, with a minor level of guidance from the research team leading the AR.

Key Words

Alternative Education, Action Research, research methods, photovoice and go-along interviews, journal writing, talanoa

Introduction

In the months prior to the COVID pandemic, lockdowns, isolation and disruption, we were an intrepid team of teachers who embarked on a unique action research (AR) project with a goal to improve teaching and learning with our Alternative Education (AE) students in New Zealand (NZ). AE is a secondary school level environment for students who have been excluded or suspended from the mainstream system. Central to our goal was our imperative to hear and understand our students' needs. Such understanding, we believed, required initially engaging with the students to hear about critical moments in their schooling experience prior to attending AE. We considered that hearing those stories – 'giving voice' to students – would enable us to better design and deliver learning experiences that were meaningful for our students. The AR project allowed us to collect stories in a 'Reconnaissance Phase' (see Figure 1), followed by deep reflection on how to enhance our teaching for learning, implement improvements, and then evaluate the impact of those improvements.

This article focuses solely on the reconnaissance – giving voice, story collection – phase of the AR. We, as four teachers in the project discuss the data collection methods we employed – photovoice, journal writing, go-along interviews and talanoa. The methods reflect the creative approaches that were fitting for our students to voice their own stories. The descriptions of the methods are in our own words also, with a little help from Eileen as our guide, along with our inquiry coaches: Hana, Judy and Adrian. In effect, we also have been 'given voice'. Before discussing the multiple methods employed, we will first provide a brief background to AE as the school context, and AR as our design.

Alternative Education

AE students are usually excluded from mainstream secondary schools in NZ as a result of multiple suspensions, exclusion, or truancy (Ministry of Education 2021). Ministry of Education (2017) data indicated that there were 5000 young people who received their education within an AE type organisation (see Schoone et al. 2022, for further background). Those young people are often labelled as failures and 'at risk'. AE centres offer opportunities for second-chance education (Gerritsen 1999) and have been described as a "refuge" (Nairn & Higgins 2011, 180) for the students. In our experience, AE teachers and co-ordinators are usually compassionate, dedicated, people who are deeply committed to turning around the lives of young people in their care. Plows and te Riele (2016) offer that the "staff are the greatest asset" (iv).

When we were asked what we, as AE teachers, would want to focus on in an AR project to improve teaching and learning for students, our call was to know our students' stories. In particular, we sought to understand the critical moments of students' schooling experiences. We felt that we often had little knowledge about our students' previous schooling or aspirations when they arrived at AE: we were encouraged to adopt a clean slate approach. We hoped that the AR might enable us to hear our students' stories of previous schooling in a safe and supportive way. Further, we believed that hearing and understanding the stories would support us in improving our approaches for interacting with, and teaching, our students. The following AR questions guided the design of this project:

1. How can teachers inquire about critical moments from students' past experiences in the formal education system?

2. How can this knowledge inform teachers' planning and pedagogy?

3. What can schools learn from the insights gained from this inquiry to improve education experiences for vulnerable students?

Action research design

In this project, the adopted AR approach conformed to the principles of inquiry learning, combining both research and change/improvement well reported in the education sector by scholars such as Adelman (1993), Carr and Kemmis (2005), and Elliott (2005). Outcomes of personal, team, organisational, and community improvement/transformation are frequently described in such AR (Somekh & Zeichner, 2009; Piggot-Irvine et al., 2021). Learning and development in our AE project was of high priority. Such thinking is reflected in our belief that:

> AR is a collaborative transformative approach with joint focus on rigorous data collection, knowledge generation, reflection and distinctive action/change elements that pursue practical solutions. … Put another way, we defined AR as having core elements of systemic research in a collaborative inquiry process that is associated with evidence-based decision making both before and after change. (Piggot-Irvine et al. 2021, 14)

We considered AR to be iterative, interactive, relational and collaborative with researchers who: "…all tell stories about the worlds they have studied" (Denzin & Lincoln 1998, 4). Students, teachers and leaders were all given voice in this project. Empowerment and emancipation to improve a social situation or condition and justice in society itself were goals (Reason & Bradbury 2008; Stringer 2007).

The model adopted in the AE project (outlined in Figure 1) is based on the work of Piggot-Irvine et al. (2021). The model has preparatory, reconnaissance, improvement/implementation, evaluation/review, reporting and further action cycles.

In the Preparatory Phase, we began by participating in professional development covering: understanding the AR process and research on AE; knowing how to 'reflect' both on and in action – a key element of AR (Brookfield 1995; Kolb 1984; Piggot-Irvine 2014; Schön 1983); and exploring and experimenting with data collection methods. A focus in the latter was on arts-based, oral, relational methods that would be appropriate for us as teachers to use for gathering stories with AE students. The following sections in this paper report on the application of those methods.

Figure 1: Action Research Design

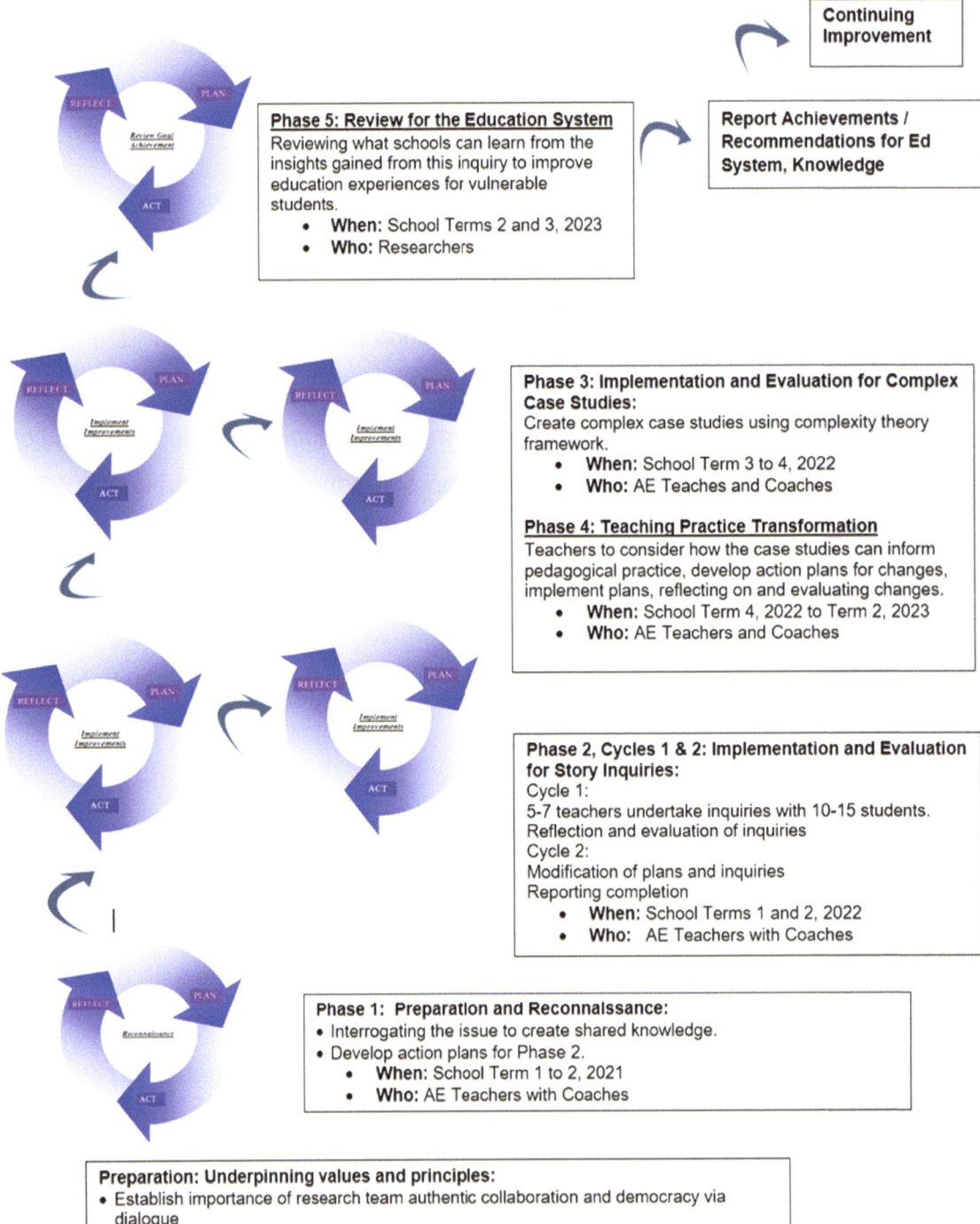

The multiple methods employed

Following the professional development workshop on relationally focused data collection methods, as teachers, we each conducted our own literature review to learn more about methods that might be suitable for our individual inquiries with students. We individually selected different methods to be used to collect stories from our AE students. In the next sections, four of us share the account of our chosen method. Our own wording and expression of the rationale for method choice and its characteristics follows.

We – as teacher action researchers in this project – were aware that our close relationship with the students might create a barrier to openness from our students. We were also conscious that giving voice might involve a risk of bringing up traumatic experiences. For this reason, we took particular care to ensure that students were aware that they could opt out of the discussion at any time. No students signalled that they needed to opt out and we feel that the methods created greater openness with our students, and deeper understanding and appreciation of them on our part – outcomes that we hoped for in our use of methods to enhance voice authenticity. The feedback we received from students following the data collection phase indicated that students felt valued and 'heard' during this process. We knew that the methods we chose were in keeping with an AR intent to limit a barrier of 'distance' between ourselves and our students. The methods chosen were designed to enhance trust (Dempsey, 2016; Garakani, 2014; Niemi, 2015). More positivistic, dispassionate, or distanced methods would not have fitted with our intent. We did not set out to be highly objective in a positivist way.

Lara Fair: Photovoice method

Why this method?

Initially, I decided to use photos/pictures in some form as I am quite a visual person myself. I wanted to create something collaboratively with the students that would represent their journey through education. I decided to use a form of photovoice called the photo-elicitation technique (Croghan et al., 2008; Hurworth et al., 2005; Sibeoni et al., 2017). The technique is often used because photography is a favoured mode of expression for youth. Interviews were conducted using images of the young person's early childhood education centres, primary, intermediate, and secondary schools as prompts. This method was selected because I felt it would help create a less formal interview environment. I recognised that the students I work with do not feel comfortable in very formal situations and using something more creative would take away that potential feeling of being cross-examined or awkward. This method helped to move the focus so it was not directly on the student. The questions and discussion became about the memories and moments provoked by the photos. Photo voice seemed like an effective distancing strategy. Such a distancing strategy is described by Niemi et al. (2015) as a "mediating tool to document and express their feelings" (610).

The interactive, collaborative, and participant-led nature of this method was the most important elements for me when working with my students (Sibeoni et al., 2017). I considered that the length of the interviews could become a problem with some students who had a shorter attention span or if there were other time constraints for adults conducting the interviews. I could not have done these interviews in a short space of time.

What I did

Prior to conducting an interview, I asked students to provide a list of any education settings they had attended from as early as they could remember. I then collated and printed out sets of photos of each of those education settings. On the day of our interview, I chose a room that was away from distractions, had nice light, and was warm and comfortable. I also provided water and snacks. I used a large table where I would have all the resources needed out and ready to use. This included coloured paper, glue, scissors, photos, and cardboard. Using the idea of a timeline (Duara et al., 2018) – another technique often used alongside photo elicitation – a chronology of the student's education journey helped to direct the discussion, as shown in the photo in Figure 2.

Figure 2: Example Student Chronology

I wanted to remove any potential barriers during this process and to achieve this I did a number of things. First, I purposefully positioned myself alongside the students on the same side of the table. I also did any writing that was needed and aided with cutting if students found it difficult. I used an open questioning technique and reflective talk to support students to delve deeper into their experiences (Dempsey et al., 2016). I was careful to ensure that the student chose the colours, the graphics, and the words. They cut the pictures out and used the pictures they wanted and left the ones out that they didn't. The selection and placement of pictures became a talking point, rather than us just talking to each other. I tried just to reaffirm what the students were saying or give them words that maybe they found hard to articulate.

My opinion of the process and outcomes

I found this process to be successful. The photos helped to provoke memories and sparked in-depth discussion and reflection on the students' education journey. Having a visual timeline was extremely useful for students to be able to look back and reflect on their educational journey so far (Duara et al., 2018).

After my first interview, I asked the student for ideas about the process and what I could change. Based on their feedback, I made an adjustment that incorporated students choosing their own critical moments after the interview process was completed. This worked very well as it ensured that the students had agency over what they saw as critical moments in their schooling.

If I were to continue using this methodology, and without the time constraints due to the COVID pandemic, I would like the students to contribute their own photos/images and even add the option of visiting schools and taking photos of their own. This approach would provide opportunities for greater involvement and ownership in the inquiry process (Farley et al., 2017).

Lydia Gray: Journal Writing

Why this method

I chose the method of journal writing after watching and being inspired by the film, *Freedom Writers* (Gruwell, 1999). I felt that the use of journaling would be a non-invasive way for my young people to express their thoughts and ideas without restriction. As Bryson (2021) suggests, "Journaling evokes mindfulness and helps writers remain present ... Journaling presents an opportunity for emotional catharsis and helps the brain regulate emotions." (99). Journal writing is a commonly used tool in AR (Frazier & Eick, 2015; Davis et al., 2018). I wanted to provide the students with an opportunity to openly and honestly share about, and release, their educational journeys while also self-reflecting on their journey and growing as individuals during the process.

What I did

I began by introducing my students to educational timelines by sharing my own educational timeline about my journey through schooling. I felt it was important to share some of my own journey and be vulnerable with my young people for them to be more open and willing to share their own with me. For me this was a critical part of the process, as I sought to establish a trusting relationship and elicit voice authenticity (Garakani, 2014).

After sharing my own journey honestly and modelling vulnerability, I invited students to draw their own educational timelines, including key people and events, and attaching emotions they felt towards these things. During this activity there were many discussions about what they felt were important moments for them and what did not really affect them in a big way.

From here, I asked them to choose one moment that particularly stood out and write about it. My young people then spent time writing, sharing and receiving feedback, allowing me to question them further to develop their ideas. Students were given several short sessions to work on their writing throughout the term, ensuring there was time to self-reflect on their writing and make any adjustments necessary. I made sure that the young people understood there were no rules in this writing. They could use whatever language and layout they felt appropriate which gave them the freedom to express themselves in their own way (Martin & Bees, 2017). This was an important part of the writing process, and my method chosen. During the process, I asked them for feedback on the journaling activity. One of the students asked if it was okay to swear. My young people wanted to know that it was okay for them to express themselves in their own voices (Garakani, 2014).

What worked

- Illustrating my own timeline helped me to model how to pick out key moments of their journeys, teachers, friends, decisions, etc. Telling them that I would never expect them to do anything that I was not prepared to do;

- The young people were able to write authentically, in their own voices. This included being able to swear and express themselves in their own words, not the words of others. They were able to write without the constraints of grammar checks and word changes;

- The young people found working on devices and typing easier than using pen and paper, allowing for easier editing by students during the process; and

- Sharing their documents with me enabled me to track their progress, offer questioning and provide feedback when they sought it; and

What did not work or impeded the use of the method

- Beginning by expecting them to handwrite their journaling. They lacked confidence off their devices and were hesitant. Reassuring, valuing them and being non-judgemental, accepting any writing errors, and allowing them to choose their own devices allowed them to be confident;

- Initially, they did not really understand what to do. This changed when I showed them my own timeline and shared my own experiences;

- Maintaining consistency in the journaling process – staff and young people were affected by sickness, class changes and attendance due to COVID; and

- Trying to fit journaling into regular classes was difficult. I needed to create a separate time for writing, a time that was focussed and uninterrupted.

My opinions on this method

I found this method to be overwhelmingly successful for not just my young people but also in my own professional development. During this process, I grew to understand that by removing parameters and rules, my young people were able to develop a greater self-awareness, grow self-understanding, and develop a greater level of self-expression through their writing (Martin & Bees, 2017).

In keeping with Utley and Garza (2011) and Martin and Bees (2017), I believe the benefit of writing promotes young people to be able to express themselves emotionally and fill gaps in their understanding of their own journey. Throughout this process, it was amazing to hear my young people talking about their experiences with each other, sharing openly about what they could have done better now that they have had time to think about and process their experiences. My young people were supportive and encouraging towards each other, while also providing constructive feedback.

Figure 3: Lydia's class at work

Overall, just having someone who actually listened and cared to hear what they thought was really powerful because I guess for a lot of them – knowing some of their home situations – they may not get listened to a lot. Others may not take the time to understand what they're thinking, what they're feeling. Being able to work with young people over time in a way where they are able to self-express, has helped to strengthen a relationship of trust and a willingness to share their journey (Garakani, 2014; Martin & Bees, 2017).

Damien Fogarty: Talanoa

A brief definition and summary of the approach

Talanoa is a Pasifika cultural concept for conversation (Vaioleti, 2006). I used talanoa in a 30–45-minute session which set the scene to create a safe space for participants through informal conversation conducted to take them on a journey. Talanoa has been used in multiple AR contexts to gather information. Cammock, Conn, and Nayar (2021), and Datta et al. (2015), for example, describe its use with Pasifika people in participatory action research.

The word talanoa is made up of two components: tala - meaning "to inform, tell, relate," and noa - meaning "of any kind, ordinary, nothing in particular" (Vaioleti, 2006, 23). So, literally, talanoa is "talking about nothing in particular, and interacting without a rigid framework" (Vaioleti, 2006, 23). My working definition is that it is a reciprocal conversation based out of relationship that was – in this context – informal. Given that many of the students I work with are Pasifika, this method was culturally appropriate.

The way the talanoa was conducted

I had an informal conversation with students who I primarily had an established relationship with. The latter was really important in terms of making participants feel emotionally safe to share. Fa'avae, Jones and Manu'atu, (2016) emphasise the importance of relationship building by suggesting that without that, conversation is at the fakatalanoa – or superficial initial meeting – level. Creating a deeper level of connection and ensuring the talanoa was a two-way exchange of sharing was critical.

I needed to create a safe space that encouraged open and honest sharing, while also ensuring the participants had an understanding that nothing would be shared without their express permission. It was also about creating a space that did not feel 'formal'. Prior to embarking on this AR, I had the privilege of speaking with a Tongan colleague who talked about how talanoa can be a space "where laughter and relationship-building can take place and trust can be built. It also is a reminder of how the most valuable conversations can take place in a setting that is not specifically designed for that purpose" (pers. comm., December 3, 2021). That is why, for the first interviews, I shared food with the participants and focussed on establishing a safe space where trust could be built. I used a combination of individual, pair, and small group talanoa. Talking to students in a group created a new dynamic and this was primarily positive.

Another key concept in talanoa, and in Pasifika cultural practice, is reciprocity. It is a two-way conversation, not just a list of pre-prescribed questions (Fa'avae, Jones & Manu'atu, 2016). My approach to this was to share, where appropriate, my own connections and experiences linked to what the students shared. An example of this was sharing my own personal experience with my daughter being bullied at school when one of the students spoke about how bullying had impacted their education journey. I hoped this displayed empathy and created a space where the young person could feel 'heard', encouraging them to share further or elaborate. Part of this process was that I was able to empathise with students, affirm their experiences and share humour and encouragement. This would not have been possible in a more rigid research framework.

Challenges

Probably the biggest challenge was the audio recording of the interviews. I made every effort to create a safe, informal, comfortable space as previously alluded to. However, especially in the beginning, the recording created 'awkwardness'. Obviously though, there is a tension between the need to collect data ethically in research and the desire to create an informal atmosphere in the talanoa. This seemed to improve as the interviews went on. As I did more interviews, I learnt ways to minimise the focus on the recording of the talanoa.

Another challenge was that the level of conversation was definitely dictated by the confidence of the students engaged in the talanoa. I attempted to ask questions that were open-ended to draw out as much information as I could. However, some participants were just more confident and eloquent than others, which obviously influenced some of the quality of data. A great example of this was that some of the most powerful reflections from one of the participants came as a result of how eloquently they expressed their experiences in education and how they were impacted by these. This particular young person is 19 years old and even just those extra couple of years of maturity definitely added to their insights and the quality of reflections.

Why talanoa was useful

Despite some challenges, the positives far outweighed any potential barriers. Subsequent to the talanoa session, I asked my students to provide comment on how they felt about the experience. The following is a quote from one student:

> For me, I enjoyed sharing my experiences though the talanoa process. I really liked that we talked about my story rather than writing it down because it felt like a conversation rather than like an exam. I have never got the opportunity before to speak freely about the situations that happened but more importantly explain how I felt. This talanoa has given me open ears so that my voice has an opportunity to be heard. It felt really cool to be a part of this, it made me feel important and that somewhere my story could be making change.

The students' reflections confirmed to me the power of talanoa as a process for open sharing (Vaioleti, 2006). My lasting impression of the talanoa process was how powerful and transformational the conversations can be. After a number of talanoa, I was left feeling very privileged at how much of the participant's personal life experiences had been shared with vulnerability and honesty. That also had the effect of professionally transforming my practice. As a Palagi (White) educator there are certain elements of my students' experiences I will never fully understand, as I have not 'walked in their shoes' (Fa'avae, Jones & Manu'atu, 2016). However, the talanoa method enabled me to look at their educational journeys through the lens of their life experiences. This cannot but help to influence and broaden my perspectives on how the institutional systems – and those of us working within them – can make change to ensure we are addressing some of the key issues that have come out of these stories. In a sense, I was an 'outsider' in terms of adopting a Pasifika methodology, but I was able to be given a glimpse inside of what it can be like for our students – many of whom have been disenfranchised and become 'outsiders' in the education system. This journey has been incredibly humbling, and I feel privileged to have been a part of all of the participants' continued journeys in education.

Figure 4: Damien in a talanoa session

Thelo Meleisea: Photo voice and 'go-along' place-based interviews

Why these methods?

I chose photo voice and 'go-along' place-based interviews because I wanted the student to feel at ease with the process and control how his story was told (Carpiano, 2009; Sutton-Brown, 2014; Wang & Burris, 1997). The data collection methods were co-constructed with the student. He was keen to participate in a research approach that blended photos, place-based reflection, and a commentary about his memorable moments in mainstream schooling before he was excluded and joined AE. Instead of doing a formal interview, we had a 'catch-up', shared food, and checked out places related to his upbringing and education around the neighbourhood where he lived. Seinfeld's TV talk show, *Comedians in cars getting coffee* (Seinfeld et al., 2012-2019), was the inspiration for the interviews. During the talk show, Seinfeld picks up a comedian and drives them to a café, where they get coffee and have an unscripted conversation. I hoped that a similar interview style in a natural setting would help the student feel more comfortable sharing his experiences.

What I did

I recruited a student for this research study who had transitioned successfully from AE to a mainstream high school. I was interested in learning about his experiences pre-AE, during AE, and post-AE as he returned to mainstream education and completed his schooling. Before we started the data collection, I met with the student after his boxing training. We got a feed from Maccas [food from McDonald's] and discussed the purpose of the research and the structure of the interviews. The plan was to conduct 45-minute interviews, truncated into shorter sessions over one afternoon.

I used a combined approach of photo voice (Sutton-Brown, 2014) and 'go-along' interviews (Carpiano, 2009). Photovoice is a participatory action research method where participants take photographs representing and illustrating their stories (Wang & Burris, 1997). I asked the student to collate/curate eight photographs from around his neighbourhood that captured his school and childhood memories.

During the go-along interviews, we visited the places he had photographed or collected/downloaded images.

In go-along interviews (Carpiano, 2009), a researcher accompanies a participant on a visit to their neighbourhood. The interview is conducted while walking, driving (or both), and the environment is the setting for the participant's story. Being on location allows the researcher to better understand the participant's experiences, while the environment acts as a prompt and assists the participant to recall experiences and memories. Our first interview was a chat in the van while we were driving to locations in the student's neighbourhood, which was designed to get the student comfortable with sharing and hanging out at key places in his educational and life journey.

During our visits and interviews at different sites, we explored themes of connection, safety, whānau (extended family) and early school life. Some of the locations we visited held positive memories for the student and highlighted times when he had felt success or connections with people and places. For example, at one place, the student had worked on a project-based learning unit that involved designing solutions for community issues. The local board accepted the design recommendations of his group and integrated their ideas into the community project development. Other locations brought up memories of good times spent with his friends and the places where they bought and shared food (see Figure 5 for an example). Visiting the school from which he was excluded allowed the student to reflect on specific highlights and lowlights from his journey in education and the 'exclusion' moment in time and context. To complete the interviews, we returned to the boxing gym, where we started the research discussion and where the student is a current member, to debrief and discuss his goals for the future.

Figure 5: An image collected by the student

My opinion of the method

I found the photo voice and go along methods worked really well for this student. He was in control throughout the process, as he was able to choose places of significance and share what he was comfortable to share (Carpiano, 2009; Sutton-Brown, 2014; Wang & Burris, 1997). Being active as we talked helped to take any pressure off, for both myself as interviewer and the student (Niemi et al., 2015). We were both in spaces that felt comfortable and familiar. I noticed that the student became more comfortable to share openly as we went through the process.

I think it was important to balance vulnerability with honouring and respecting where the student was at. I could tell by his body language where he was at as well as by how much information he shared. I knew that there was a whole lot more that he was not saying, and that was totally fine, and as it should be, because it was his choice how much he shared (Dempsey, et al 2016; Tilley & Taylor, 2018).

Following the interviews, I edited videos of the process and shared these with the student and invited further thoughts from him. This worked well as he could see and reflect again, and share some fresh perspectives. When asked what he thought of the research methods, he said:

> It was good to help Thelo with future AE kids coming through the system. I liked that we went back to places that meant a lot to me. It was more like hanging out and remembering the good times...yo with a phat feed and yeah maybe some of the dark times when I first got kicked out of school. I know now that if this can help make schools better for kids like me then yeah, use it.

Overall, I would recommend this method to others, but it is a time-consuming process, so making allowances for this is important. A combination of photo-voice and 'go along' interviews provided a focus for our conversations. Being on the move and reflecting helped to create a safe space for sharing with a medium (places) as the focus.

Conclusion

The purpose of this research was to consider how we as teachers can inquire about critical moments from students' past experiences in the formal education system. The focus of this paper is solely on the implementation of relationally oriented data collection methods that enable 'giving voice' to students. We believe that the methods were very successful in giving voice to our students, as well as to us as teachers. Our students have experienced significant challenges in education and consequently are often reluctant to share critical moments of their schooling experiences with others. The methods we chose were interactive, compassionate, and *enabled* responsiveness from our students. Further, the writing of this paper has also given us voice to express how we have experienced the methods.

As we reflected together on our chosen methods, we recognised certain themes emerging. We all shared a similar desire to ensure a safe environment that was conducive to the sharing of experiences. We sought to do this through a range of strategies including interactive processes and ethical relationship building. Interactive processes we used included material objects such as food, photos and photo boards, writing and go-along experiences. These distancing strategies serve as a kind of mediating tool between the students and ourselves as teacher-researchers (Niemi et al., 2015). We all noticed that the distancing strategies served as a focus, not directly on the students but indirectly, as tools for focused and rich conversations. These findings are consistent with Tilley and Taylor (2018) noting that the use of "visual methods may create opportunities to generate new knowledge and access youths' different memories of their experiences" (2189).

Additionally, we emphasised the importance of knowing the students, or having previously established relationships with them that were based on empathy, care and acceptance. Ensuring students felt 'at ease' was of upmost importance. A strength of this AR project was that we already had relationship with the students with whom we were inquiring with. This is in contrast to other studies where researchers have struggled within a limited period of time to develop safe and trusting relationships, especially with vulnerable populations, including disenfranchised young people (Dempsey et al., 2016; Garakani, 2014; Gombert et al., 2016; Tilley & Taylor, 2018). By contrast, we were able to create spaces which were safe and enabled rich and meaningful conversations about schooling experiences.

Creating a safe space for meaningful conversations was also in part enabled through reciprocal sharing of personal stories (Dempsey et al., 2016; Fa'avae, Jones & Manu'atu, 2016). We were willing early in the data collection process, to share openly about our own schooling experiences. By revealing something personal from our own lives, we showed a level of respectful and ethical openness and vulnerability. As an interviewing approach, Dempsey et al. (2016) have found similarly that this reciprocity serves to foster rapport between researchers and participants.

When asked how our students experienced our chosen methods and the research processes, they acknowledged feeling heard, appreciated the opportunities for self-expression, and hoped that their voice and story might impact change. While each of us intentionally sought interactive processes that were mediating tools (Niemi et al., 2015), we also intentionally employed aspects of therapeutic interviewing such as empathic listening, reflective talk and acceptance of narratives without judgement (Dempsey et al., 2016). These combined approaches contributed to our students' experiences of feeling heard.

In our readying to embark on the Implementation Phase of our AR journey, we have deeply analysed the content of the stories our students provided. The results of that analysis will be reported in our next paper, but briefly, we can report that the methods we have described in this paper generated considerable data to help inform how we could improve our teaching and the learning for students. In short, we have been prepared for 'informed' improvement: an underpinning element of AR.

Funding details

This work was supported by the Teaching and Learning Research Initiative, New Zealand under Grant number 9204.

Disclosure statement

The authors report there are no competing interests to declare.

References

Adelman, C. 1993. "Kurt Lewin and the Origins of Action Research." *Educational Action Research, 1* (1): 7–24. https://doi.org/10.1080/0965079930010102.

Brookfield, S. 1995. *Becoming a Critically Reflective Teacher*. San Francisco, CA: Jossey-Bass.

Bryson, D. 2021. "Continuing Professional Development and Journaling." *Journal of Visual Communication in Medicine*, 44 (4): 198-200.

Cammock, R., C. Conn, and S. Nayar. 2021. "Strengthening Pacific Voices through Talanoa Participatory Action Research." *AlterNative: An International Journal of Indigenous Peoples*, 17 (1): 120–129. https://doi.org/10.1177/1177180121996321

Carpiano, R. M. 2009. "Come Take a Walk With Me: The 'Go-Along' Interview as a Novel Method for Studying the Implications of Place for Health and Well-being". *Health & Place*, 15 (1): 263-272.

Carr, W., and S. Kemmis. 2005. "Staying Critical." *Educational Action Research, 13* (3): 347–58. doi: 10.1080/09650790500200296.

Croghan, R., C. Griffin, J. Hunter, and A. Phoenix. 2008. "Young People's Constructions of Self: Notes on the Use and Analysis of the Photo-Elicitation Methods." *International Journal of Social Research Methodology, 11* (4): 345-356.

Datta R., N.U. Khyang, H.K.P. Khyang, H.A.P. Kheyang, M.C. Khyang, and J. Chapola. 2015. "Participatory Action Research and Researcher's Responsibilities: An Experience with an Indigenous Community". *International Journal of Social Research Methodology, 18* (6): 581–599. https://doi.org/10.1080/13645579.2014.927492

Davis, J., C. Clayton, and J. Broome. 2018. "Thinking Like Researchers: Action Research and its Impact on Novice Teachers' Thinking." *Educational Action Research, 26*, 59–74. doi: 10.1080/09650792.2017.1284012

Dempsey, L., M. Dowling, P. Larkin and K. Murphy. 2016. "Sensitive Interviewing in Qualitative Research." *Research in Nursing & Health, 39*: 480-490.

Denzin, N. K., & Yvonne S. Lincoln. 1998. *Strategies of Qualitative Inquiry: Handbook of Qualitative Research.* London: Sage Publications.

Duara, R., S. Hugh-Jones, and A. Madill. 2018. "Photo-Elicitation and Time-Lining to Enhance the Research Interview: Exploring the Quarterlife Crisis of Young Adults in India and the United Kingdom". *Qualitative Research in Psychology, 19* (1): 131–124. https://doi.org/10.1080/14780887.2018. 1545068

Elliott, J. 2005. "Becoming Critical: The Failure to Connect". *Educational Action Research, 13* (3): 359–374. doi: 10.1080/09650790500200297.

Fa'avae, D., A. Jones, and L. Manu'atu. 2016. "Talanoa'i 'a e Talanoa — Talking About Talanoa: Some Dilemmas of a Novice Researcher". *AlterNative 12* (2): 138–150.

Farley, L. A., K. Brooks and K. Popek. 2017. "Engaging Students in Praxis Using Photo-Voice Research". *Multicultural Education, 24* (2): 49-54.

Frazier, L. C., and C. Eick. 2015. "Approaches to Critical Reflection: Written and Video Journaling". *Reflective Practice. 16*, 575–594. doi: 10.1080/14623943.2015.1064374

Garakani, T. 2014. "Young People Have a Lot to Say…With Trust, Time and Tools: The Voices of Inuit Youth in Nunavik." *Canadian Journal of Education 31* (1): 234-257.

Gerritsen, J. 1999. "An Educated Alternative." *New Zealand Education Gazette, 78* (14): 4–9.

Gombert, K., F. Douglas, K. McArdle, and S. Carlisle. 2016. "Reflections on Ethical Dilemmas in Working with So-Called 'Vulnerable' and 'Hard-to-Reach' Groups: Experiences from the Foodways and Futures Project." *Educational Action Research, 24*: 583-597. https://doi.org/10.1080/09650792.2015.1106958.

Gruwell, E. 1999. *The Freedom Writers Diary: How a Teacher and 150 Teens Used Writing to Change Themselves and the World Around Them.* New York: Broadway Books.

Hurworth, R., E. Clark, J. Martin, and S. Thomsen. 2005. "The Use of Photo-Interviewing: Three Examples from Health Evaluation and Research." *Evaluation Journal of Australasia, 4* (1-2): 52-62.

Kolb, D. 1984. *Experiential Learning: Experience as the Source of Learning and Development.* Englewood Cliffs, NJ: Prentice Hall.

Martin, J. L. and J. A. Bees. 2017. "Talking Back at School: Using the Literacy Classroom as a Site for Resistance to the School - to Prison Pipeline and Recognition of Students Labelled 'At-Risk'." *Urban Education 52* (10): 1204-1232.

Ministry of Education. 2017. Factors Associated with the Risk of Not Achieving in Education. https://www.education.govt.nz/our-work/information-releases/information-releases-2012-2017/factors-associated-with-the-risk-of-not-achieving-ineducation/.

Ministry of Education. 2021. Alternative Education Provision. https://alternativeeducation.tki.org.nz/Alternative-education

Nairn, K., and J. Higgins. 2011. "The Emotional Geographies of Neoliberal School Reforms: Spaces of Refuge and Containment." *Emotion, Space and Society 4*: 180–186. doi:10.1016/j.emospa. 2010.10.001.

Niemi, R., K. Kumpulainen, and L. Lipponen. 2015. "Pupil's Documentation Enlightening Teachers' Practical Theory and Pedagogical Actions." *Educational Action Research 23* (4): 599-614.

Piggot-Irvine, E. 2014. "Critical Reflection." In *Encyclopedia of Action Research*, edited by David Coghlan & Mary Brydon-Miller, 225-231. London: SAGE. doi: http://dx.doi.org/10.4135/9781446294406.n97

Piggot-Irvine, E., L. Ferkins, W. Rowe, and S. Sankaran. 2021. *The Evaluative Study of Action Research: Rigorous Findings on Process and Impact from Around the World.* Australia: Routledge Taylor and Francis.

Plows, Vicky, and Kitty te Riele. 2016. *Professional Learning in Flexible Learning Programs.* Melbourne: The Victoria Institute for Education, Diversity and Lifelong Learning.

Reason, P., and Hilary. Bradbury. 2008. *The Handbook of Action Research: Participative Inquiry and Practice* (2nd ed.). Thousand Oaks: Sage Publications.

Schön, D. 1983. *The Reflective Practitioner: How Professionals Think in Action.* New York, NY: Basic Books.

Schoone, A., J. Bruce, E. Piggot-Irvine, and H. Turner-Adams. 2022. "How Alternative Education Teachers Embarked on Getting to the Heart of Young People's Schooling Stories." *International Journal of Inclusive Education.* https://doi.org/10.1080/13603116.2022.2119289

Seinfeld, J., G. Shapiro, M. Gastgaber, and T. Johnston. 2012-2019. *Comedians in Cars Getting Coffee* [TV series]. Barry Katz Entertainment. Columbus 81 Productions: Embassy Row, Sony Pictures Television.

Sibeoni, J., E. Costa-Drolon, and L. Poulmarc'h. et al. (2017). "Photo-elicitation with Adolescents in Qualitative Research: An Example of its Use in Exploring Family Interactions in Adolescent Psychiatry." *Child Adolescent Psychiatry Mental Health, 11* (49). https://doi.org/10.1186/s13034-017-0186-z

Somekh, B., and K. Zeichner. 2009. "Action Research for Educational Reform: Remodelling Action Research Theories and Practices in Local Contexts." *Educational Action Research, 17* (1): 5–21. https://doi.org/10.1080/09650790802667402.

Stringer, E. T. 2007. *Action Research.* 3rd ed. Thousand Oaks: Sage Publications.

Sutton-Brown, C. A. 2014. "Photovoice: A Methodological Guide." *Photography and Culture, 7* (2): 169-185.

Tilley, S. and Taylor, L. 2018. "Qualitative Methods and Respectful Praxis: Researching with Youth." *The Qualitative Report 23 (9):* 2184-2204. https://doi.org/10.46743/2160-3715/2018.3482.

Utley, A. and Garza, Y. 2011. "The Therapeutic Use of Journaling with Adolescents." *Journal of Creativity in Mental Health, (6)* 1: 29-41.

Vaioleti, T. M. 2006. "Talanoa Research Methodology: A Developing Position on Pacific Research." *Waikato Journal of Education, 12,* 21-34.

Wang, C., and M. A. Burris. 1997. "Photovoice: Concept, Methodology, and Use for Participatory Needs Assessment." *Health Education & Behavior, 24* (3): 369-387.

Action Learning, Action Research Association

The Action Learning, Action Research Association Ltd (ALAR Association, also known as ALARA) is a global network of programs, institutions, professionals, and people interested in using Action Learning and Action Research to generate collaborative learning, training, research and action to transform workplaces, schools, colleges, universities, communities, voluntary organisations, governments and businesses.

ALAR Association's vision is to create a more equitable, just, joyful, productive, peaceful and sustainable society by promoting local and global change through the wide use of Action Learning and Action Research by individuals, groups and organisations.

ALAR Association provides information and networking for researchers and practitioners, a peer-reviewed journal, this Monograph series and other publications, webinars, conferences and world congresses. It also supports professional development of practitioners and research activities. You can find out more about ALAR Association at https://www.alarassociation.org/ or about the *Action Learning and Action Research Journal* at https://alarj.alarassociation.org/.

Printed by Libri Plureos GmbH in Hamburg, Germany